ROAMING DOGS

A Howling Storm

Jared Bailey

To my loving parents, Daniel and Karell, for always encouraging my dreams and my Greenwood friends and teachers for inspiring and supporting me.

TABLE OF CONTENTS

PROLOGUE

The dogs and wolves were howling fiercely. Silverstone picked up her pup and ran silently toward the camp entrance. *How did it get like this?* She thought. *How did I lead my pack to war?* A startling howl frightened her. Two dogs were heading straight toward her. "Silverstone, we're losing the battle. What are we going to do?" One of them asked.

Silverstone sighed and sat down her pup at the brown dog's feet. "Take care of Moon, she needs all the care she can get."

The brown dog nodded, picked up Moon, and flicked her tail for all the dogs to follow. Silverstone gave Moon and the brown dog a swift lick, then ran back into the camp.

Wolves quickly surrounded her, and she was clawed to shreds. But they didn't kill her. Instead, they took her to a dark hole, which led deeper and deeper into the earth. The wolves shoved her down the hole and she watched in pain as they covered the hole with prey bones.

CHAPTER 1

Moon awoke to the sound of distant barks. She got up, extended her paws, and arched her back into a long, comfortable stretch. She shook out her long, gray fur and stepped outside the Recruit's den into the sunlight. Everyone in the pack was awake now. She spotted Sunnystorm and wagged her tail happily.

When she approached her, she could hear her talking to the pack's Beta, Fangtooth. "Good morning, Sunnystorm!" Moon said happily with her tongue lolling out of her mouth. Sunnystorm looked at her, a glint of warmth in her steady blue gaze. "Moon, if you wouldn't mind, I need you to lead a hunting party. The prey pile is running low."

Moon nodded seriously and left them to their conversation. What *should I bring? I've never led a hunting party!* Moon looked around the camp and saw Winterpelt and Boltwing sharing a squirrel. *Bingo,* she thought.

+++

Moon padded along the stream's edge with Winterpelt and Boltwing following close behind. She was on high alert for any sound or scent of prey creatures moving near the water.

A strong breeze carried the scent of rabbit somewhere nearby. If they could catch a fat rabbit or two, that would be a huge improvement to the prey pile. She followed the scent, leaving the stream, and found herself staring across wide, open moorland. Rabbits loved to make their burrows here. She glanced behind her to see that the two other dogs noticed it, too. If they planned on catching one, they needed to depend on stealth. It wasn't long until four plump-looking rabbits came into sight. The grass here was shorter than the grass in the forest and there weren't many trees in this area, but at least there were plenty of rabbits.

Moon crouched down so low that her stomach rubbed against the ground. She tried her best to stay out of sight and hoped that her gray pelt would not give her away. Making sure that her scent was downwind, she signaled with her tail for Boltwing to take the nearest rabbit from the right and Winterpelt to take it from the left. The mates took their position and Moon began to creep closer to the rabbit. It sniffed around, but it didn't seem to notice Moon or the other dog's presence. She crept closer, and closer, and then leaped. It noticed her and turned and dashed for the nearest hole. "No!" Moon shouted angrily.

She began the chase but before she could reach it, Winterpelt jumped out of her hiding spot and killed the rabbit with a bite to the neck. Boltwing rustled out through the grass, a rabbit dangling in his jaws. Moon sat down on her haunches, defeat washing over her. *Now I'm going to return to the pack empty-handed.* "Do not be discouraged, young one," Winterpelt said, giving her a swift lick on the ear. "We still have two big rabbits. That will hold the pack for now."

"That's why we're here," Boltwing added. Moon shook herself from head to tail and got up. They began their journey back to camp, Moon taking up the rear. They traveled beside the small stream, still sniffing for any prey. A disgusting smell entered her snout and she barked. It smelled like some animal was decaying. Winterpelt and Boltwing turned back toward her, both wearing a confused expression.

When they did, they shook their heads in disgust. Moon followed the fowl scent to a log. Hidden inside of it was a weasel. It looked as if it had been there for at least five moons. Moon reluctantly pulled it out of the log and dropped it in front of them. Boltwing and Winterpelt dropped their rabbits to examine the weasel. Boltwing approached it carefully and sniffed it. He jumped back and stared back at Winterpelt and Moon. "Wolves." He said, staring at the rotten prey. "This was eaten by wolves." It felt as if the whole world was crashing down on Moon. *Could it be?* She thought. *Could my other pack be hunting in this forest?*

Moon was half dog, half wolf. When she was younger, Sunnystorm told her about her noble mother and how she died to save her pack. But no matter how many times she would ask, she would not tell her about her father.

"We must tell Sunnystorm about this at once," Winterpelt added, interrupting her thoughts. They rushed back to camp. Winterpelt and Boltwing dropped their rabbits into the pile and rushed to Sunnystorm and Fangtooth's den. Moon's eyes began to feel heavy. Her mind was so caught on the decayed prey that she hadn't even noticed that the sun was beginning to set. Moon trotted towards the Recruit's Den and settled down. The pack's Omega, Cometfire, must have switched out the moss bedding. It felt softer than her old one. It didn't take that long for sleep to flood over her.

CHAPTER 2

Moon awoke the next day drowsy. She groomed her ruffled fur and stepped out of the den. She trotted toward the prey pile and gulped down a squirrel.

"Hello, young one," said Sunnystorm, startling Moon. She smiled awkwardly and gulped down the last remains of the squirrel. "I've heard about the wolf scent that your patrol found."

Moon scrambled to her feet to face her. "I have nothing to do with this, honest!" Sunnystorm laughed and looked back at her. "Of course not, I wouldn't think anything of it. But I would like you to join the morning patrol. If there is a wolf pack in the area, we need to chase them off before this gets too out of hand." Then, she grabbed a vole out of the pile and disappeared into her den. Moon sighed gratefully and let her neck fur lie down. She could see some dogs gathering at the entrance to the camp.

She spotted Blaze, her best friend, in the group and rushed toward him. She greeted him with a swift lick on the head. Ever since Sunnystorm had brought Moon into the pack, they became immediate friends, though Blaze was older than her.

The group exited the camp and set off through the forest. So many prey scents flooded into her nose. She knew she was not allowed to eat until they got back, but the squirrel she ate this morning wasn't enough for her growing hunger. She peaked ahead from the back of the group to see if anyone was watching her. Fangtooth was leading the patrol down a river, paying no attention to Moon. She waited a few seconds before dashing into the undergrowth. Almost immediately the smell of vole rushed up her scent glands.

She positioned her ears perfectly to try and pinpoint the position of it. It wasn't long until it was in her line of sight. She crouched down and began to stalk the creature. The vole must've scented her, because it stopped moving and began running. But by then, it was too late. Almost as soon as it noticed her, she had begun the chase. She was too fast for it, so she swiftly pawed it to the ground and finished it with a victorious bite.

The patrol would notice that she was gone by now, so she had to finish this quickly. She took one bite of it and sighed. It tasted so good. Then, she felt her fur prickle in fear. She turned around and saw two amber eyes staring straight at her. Instinctively, she growled. The pair of eyes disappeared and there was no trace of a scent. She shrugged and began to take another bite of the vole when she was knocked over by a heavy force. Great paws slammed into her side, racking the fur off it. Moon yowled in pain as her attacker bit their needle-sharp teeth into her neck. Moon tried her best to not struggle. That would make the teeth dig deeper into the skin. She went limp. She stayed as still as possible. Her attacker loosened their grip on her, but their paws stayed like boulders. "Well, it's just one of those weak little pups. I think I can take one of these." They began to dig their teeth back in. This is when she would strike. Moon wriggled under the attacker's paws, surprising them and making the paws loosen their grip. Then, she rolled over and scrambled to her paws. It was now clear who was attacking her. A large, muscular gray body was breathing heavily. A wolf.

She growled, accepting the challenge. Moon leaped at the wolf and landed straight on her back. She began to dig her claws into her shoulders. Now it was her turn to yowl. The wolf threw her off and bit down on her tail. Moon was furious. Her teeth were enclosed on the wolf's hind leg. She bit down as hard as she could until the wolf let go of her tail and dropped to the ground, whimpering.

Moon saw the look of pain in the wolf's eyes and had sympathy for her. Moon looked down at the half-eaten vole and nudged it toward her. The wolf looked up at her and snarled, "I don't need to be fed, pup." But she took one look at the vole and finished it in two big bites.

Moon gave an amused bark and sat down. "I guess I can thank you for that, but if it wasn't for you, I wouldn't have to have a pup feed me!" Moon ignored her insult and looked at her wound. "That wound looks nasty. Sorry about that. Maybe if I took you to my healer, you would feel better."

"I don't need to go to your so-called 'pack' to be healed. I'm Thornstripe, one of StormPack's strongest warriors!" Moon tilted her head in confusion. "StormPack?" She echoed. "Yes. You're a little young to be deaf," she snapped.

Just then, there was a rustling in the bushes. A muscular figure jumped out from it and landed right on the wolf. She yelped in surprise as all her weight was put on her leg. Then recognition washed over Moon. It was Fangtooth.

CHAPTER 3

"What is the meaning of this?" Growled Fangtooth. Moon shrank back in fear. The rest of the patrol emerged from the bushes and gaped at the scene. "I'm waiting." He was staring straight at her now, his green eyes blazing. "She attacked me." Moon whimpered. "I gave her a wound that hurt her a lot. I felt bad for doing it so I—" Moon took a big gulp before continuing. "I fed her."

Fangtooth curled his lips back into a menacing snarl. Moon could see where he got his name from. His long fangs glinted in the sunlight. Blaze shot a worried glance toward Moon.

"At least we have a prisoner now," said Talonfoot, a tan-furred Roamer excitedly. Fangtooth nodded his agreement and grabbed Thornstripe by her scruff and dragged her back to camp.

Moon walked nervously into the clearing. A pup ran outside of the nursery curiously toward the returning dogs. "Who's that?" She shouted. "And why is she so *big!*" Fangtooth sent her away with a flick of his tail. As if he had signaled her, Sunnystorm strode out of her den. She spotted the patrol and came to greet them.

"I see we have caught a rogue," she stated calmly. She watched Thornstripe with a hungering curiosity. "Bring her to my den." Then, she walked across the clearing to speak with the pup's mother. Moon sighed in relief as Fangtooth strolled away toward the prey pile. *He must have forgotten about my punishment,* she thought.

Moon trotted happily toward the prey pile herself and began to pull out a marmot from the pile when Fangtooth stopped her with a snarl. "You have already eaten; you certainly don't need more." Moon lowered her head in obedience and went to the Recruit's Den. Blaze was in there grooming himself. He stopped and looked up when Moon entered.

"What were you thinking?" He exclaimed. "Feeding the enemy, that was nuts!" Moon sat beside him and sighed. "I know it was the wrong thing, but she was hurt! I couldn't let an innocent dog die."

"Innocent!?" Blaze cried out, but lowered his voice when Ruby, a short-haired female with gray fur, began to stir from where she slept soundly in her mossy bed. "That wolf is part of a pack that doesn't care about us dogs! They stole our prey, and she even attacked you!" Moon lowered her head. "Not all wolves are bad." She mumbled.

Blaze began to apologize when Sunnystorm entered the den. "Moon, I would like to speak to you in my den please." And without another word, she turned and left. Moon looked at Blaze helplessly, but he only sighed and turned his head.

Moon walked toward Sunnystorms's den with her head low. She passed Skystar, a white-haired dog, who snickered teasingly. When she reached her den, she smelled the familiar scent of wolf. She peeked inside of the den to see Sunnystorm sitting with her bushy brown tail over her front paws. And sitting in the very back of the den was Thornstripe.

"Come join us, Moon." She said coolly. Moon stepped nervously into the warm den. Moon had only been in this den once. But that was when she was a pup and Sunnystorm was raising her.

Moon sat down near Thornstripe. The wolf scooted a few inches away from her and raised her snout defensively. "I apologize for hunting in your territory. But I had to find a place to eat to survive. This pup has nothing to do with this and she should not be punished for showing empathy." Sunnystorm raised her brow, amused. Moon gave Thornstripe a thankful glance and she returned with a quick nod. "I was not going to punish her," said Sunnystorm

"But," Sunnystorm continued, "That was not the reason she was brought here. I wanted to talk to both of you about finding this wolf pack." Moon's ears pricked up curiously. *Why would she pick me?* As if reading her thoughts, Sunnystorm calmly said, "You are a skilled fighter. And you are part wolf; they might trust you." Moon nodded in understanding.

"You will set off at once." Sunnystorm turned her fiery glare toward Thornstripe. "I know I can trust you to take care of this young one."

Thornstripe dipped her head respectfully and stood. "Come, young Recruit. We have work to do." And with that, they exited the camp.

CHAPTER 4

Moon sniffed the forest floor intently. Thornstripe seemed to know where she was going, but Moon had no idea. She had never been to this part of the forest before. She squelched in the mud beneath her paws. Not much sunlight got through to this part of the forest.

Thornstripe stopped walking suddenly and crouched down. She flicked her tail toward Moon to do the same. Quickly, she awkwardly crouched down as four gray wolves bigger than her stomped past their hiding spot. When they passed, they set off again.

Moon spotted a ravine up ahead of them. It was engulfed in the scent of wolves. They were all doing some kind of job. Different wolves entered the camp, prey dangling from their large jaws.

Moon gaped at the sight of seeing that they looked very well fed. All of them had full bellies and they all looked healthy, unlike BreezePack.

Thornstripe glanced in Moon's direction. "Don't turn them into your idols just because of the way they look. They are cruel inside. They will do anything to keep their pack strong. And I mean *anything.*"

Thornstripe turned toward the entrance to the camp. A returning hunting patrol spotted them and growled. "Well, well, well, if it isn't Thornstripe, our little traitor. I see you've come back for some more wounds." Then the wolf glanced in Moon's direction. "And this time you're not doing it alone." He gave a sly smile and then herded them into the camp. Almost as soon as they entered, they were swarmed by wolves. Some of them teased, some of them daring to claw them to shreds. Moon's fur bristled anxiously at a horrifying sight. A wolf bigger than any wolf she'd seen stomped toward them. Alarmed and in shock, she leaped toward him. He swatted her away like a squirrel and pinned her to the ground. His eyes were a dark green and his fangs glinted in the light.

"Well, it looks like we have a puny little dog in our pack. And we have some more food to store."

The other wolves began to laugh with their fangs bared. They snarled and growled at her. Thornstripe stepped in front of her protectively. "You said that she was a puny weak *dog*. Well, Stormfoot, I'd like you to know that she is one of us."

Moon winced. She hadn't expected Thornstripe to tell her Pack about her wolf heritage. But it was a good distraction. She had all the wolves' attention now. The wolf named Stormfoot stared at her with ferocious eyes. "What do you mean she's one of us?"

Thornstripe chuckled a laugh. "She's part wolf. I'm not sure who her parents were, but they must have been foolish." Moon tried to hold back a growl in her throat. How could she say that? *Whoever my parents were, they must have abandoned me for a good reason. If I'm a good dog, they must be good too. Right?*

"So," Thornstripe went on, "you should treat her with the same respect any wolf would get." Some of the wolves surrounding them looked thoughtful. Others continued to stare with full hostility and hatred. Stormfoot, though, had the strongest glare. Moon almost wanted to run back to the safety of her own pack. But something deep inside told her not to.

Thornstripe looked calmly into Stormfoot's eyes, while he returned it with a growl. "I will release her, but you must be punished. I told you if you came back, you'd pay. And I see you didn't get the message." Thornstripe pricked her ears up in surprise. "You never said that! You told me to hunt in the dog's territory for the pack! I didn't know you were exiling me!" Within the blink of an eye, three wolves had already tackled her. There was a writhing ball of gray fur wrestling on the sandy ground. Thornstripe had latched her teeth on the leg of one of the attackers and blood began dripping, mending with the sand.

Moon didn't know what to do. Fight for a rogue dog or flee to the safety of her pack. Thornstripe wasn't going to be able to win the fight alone. Moon leaped into the battle. She grabbed onto the scruff of a wolf with a scarred eye and dragged him away.

He whipped around, loosening her grip. He then jumped on top of Moon, the extra weight making her drop to the ground. Moon could feel the sharp fangs of the wolf piercing her neck.

She panicked and wriggled helplessly under her attacker. Her eyes began to cloud, and she could feel herself getting weaker. With one final struggle, she went limp, and the clearing drifted away into darkness.

CHAPTER 5

Moon looked around curiously. She was in a clearing surrounded by four blue-glowing large rocks. It looked as if shards of the moon had fallen from the sky. There was a faint whisper that seemed to be coming from everywhere.

Moon whipped around to find a dog way bigger than her gazing intently down at her. She looked old and frail, but at the same time looked like she could take Moon out with a touch of her claw.

The dog approached her with gentle steps. Moon shrank back with a warning growl. Something about this dog made Moon undeniably scared. As the dog got closer, a wave of calmness washed over Moon. All her suspicions had just gone away. Like it was never there. The strange dog touched noses with her, and Moon felt a whiff of strength surging through her. Her eyes shot open. She was still in the wolf camp, but now there were more dogs in the camp. Breezepack! She recognized the black fur of Fangtooth. He was wrestling with Stormfoot. With new energy now surging through her paws, she leaped up and grabbed the scruff of a young Roamer.

Startled, the wolf easily fell to the ground where Moon was able to scar their flank.

The camp was a flurry of red and brown and gray fur. It was chaos. But Moon could clearly see; that Breezepack was winning. The wolves began running for cover eventually. Moon could barely hide her excitement. Fangtooth quickly gathered everyone, and they left the camp. Thornstripe, she noticed, was also with them. She too had the wounds of battle.

Moon slowed her step so she could pace beside her. "Are you hurt?" Moon asked. Thornstripe sighed. "The wounds of others' words burn deeper than the wounds of a battle." She walked ahead of Moon towards Fangtooth, who seemed calmer toward her than before. Moon wondered what had changed. And better yet, what would happen next?

Moon blinked three times fast. The forest was dark, and she could not see any signs of life. There was a faint blue light in the distance.

She heard growling behind her and turned to see a pair of red eyes glaring at her. Startled, she dashed off toward the light. But the farther she ran, the farther the light went. Then, Moon began to finally approach it.

She leaped toward it only to find herself falling into a bottomless pit. She landed painfully on her side, wheezing. The two glowing eyes pierced through her fur. But the blue light was back, and this time in the form of a dog. Moon heard the soft whisper of it say, "You must fight your fear. If you don't, then you will lead your pack to doom." Almost as fast as it appeared, it was gone. The two red eyes had multiplied into millions surrounding her. All staring straight at Moon.

She woke up in a cold sweat. The light was streaming into the den. Moon realized she had clawed her bedding to shreds. She began her morning routine.

After she finished stretching, she left the den. Fangtooth was sending out the morning patrols. And Sunnystorm was on her back, taking in the warmth of the sun. Moon decided to talk to her.

Sunnystorm seemed to sense her approach, for she said, "Moon, perfect timing. I'd like to speak with you."

Sunnystorm got up, stretched, and entered her den. Moon followed behind more slowly. *What does she want from me? Is she going to talk to me about the battle, or Thornstripe? What if it's neither, and I'm in trouble for a different reason?*

Sunnystorm settled down in her neatly made bedding, making room for Moon to lay beside her. "I just want you to know, you're not in trouble. I have good news." Moon's heart pounded even more. "I'd like to name you as a full-fledged Roamer of this pack. You have shown your loyalty and strength in battle and Breezepack will honor you for it."

Moon bowed her head in thanks, then exited the den. Blaze was waiting outside the den. "Congratulations!" He said excitedly. Graycloud trotted up to the two Recruits. "I hear someone is becoming a Roamer." Graycloud was a sweet dog. He is strong, loyal, and very wise. Moon would always turn to him for help when she was a little pup. Graycloud was also Blaze's trainer.

"I hope you live a beautiful life as a Roamer," he continued. "One day, you might even lead this pack yourself."

Moon stared at him, lost in thought. *Is he trying to tell me something? Does he see something I don't?*

Sunnystorm emerged from her den and dismissed the two dogs with a flick of her tail. Then, she called, "Dogs of Breezepack, gather around for a meeting."

Dogs immediately began filing out of their dens, circling Sunnystorm. "We are gathered here today to recognize one of these dogs. Moon, step up." Moon felt her fur prickling in fear as she walked to the front of the crowd. The memory of her dream crowded into her mind. All the blazing eyes staring at her. Moon was staring absentmindedly, so she didn't realize that Sunnystorm had asked her something.

"Do you promise to serve this pack for as long as you live, no matter what the cost?" She repeated. Moon nodded shakily, the glowing dog's words repeating in her head. *You must fight your fear. If you don't, you will lead your pack to doom.* "Then with the power vested in me, I give you your Roamer name. Moon, you will now be known as Moonheart." And just like that, howls broke out from outside the camp.

CHAPTER 6

Wolves piled in through the camp entrance shouting, "Revenge!" Moonheart was the first to react. She charged toward Stormfoot. "Stop! Please!" She skidded to a stop as the big dog swiped a paw at her. "Why should we? You raided our camp! Not to mention you scared away all our prey." He leaped toward Moonheart, but she was able to dodge with ease.

The rest of the pack stared in awe as the wolves surrounded them. Fangtooth's fur bristled with anger as a wolf swatted at him. But they didn't get away without a claw to the face. Sunnystorm stood tall, glaring at the wolves. "If you have something to say," she said, "speak with your words. Not with your teeth."

Stormfoot pushed past Moonheart to stand in front of Sunnystorm. She was the size of a Recruit compared to Stormfoot. "Well then, let's talk privately. Your Beta may come as well."

Sunnystorm, Fangtooth, and Stormfoot walked towards Sunnystorm's den and soon disappeared. Thornstripe emerged from the Healer's den with Bluepetal following close behind. Bluepetal was the pack's Healer and also, yet another dog Moonheart looked up to.

Thornstripe took one glance at the mess, and completely lost it. She leaped at the nearest Roamer and pinned them down. "Where is he? Where is Stormfoot!" Moonheart quickly knocked her off the wolf and explained what had happened. When she finished, Thornfoot looked toward Sunnystorm's den, shocked.

Like she had been called, Sunnystorm emerged from the den. She signaled with her tail for Bluepetal to come. They murmured together for a few moments and then walked toward the Healer's den. *What? That's it? You just disappear into the den, talk for a while, then just walk off? What's going on?* Stormfoot came out of the den shortly after. But where was Fangtooth? The wolf pack settled at the other side of the clearing. They seemed to be waiting for something.

Moonheart looked around, then headed for the den. "Ah ah ah," Stormfoot said, approaching her. "I need you for something else. Fetch us some prey. Your Alpha was going to do it, but she seemed to have put that to the side."

Moonheart sighed, took a final glance at the den, and then walked to the prey pile. It was empty except for a squirrel, two rabbits, and a vole. None of those would feed the whole wolf pack. Winter was approaching, and all the prey in the forest was scrawny. *With the pack barely holding on, how can we afford to give away precious prey to another pack?* Then, Moonheart had an idea. If she went hunting, she could investigate their camp. And maybe even actually catch some decent prey.

She looked around the camp to see if anyone was watching, then dashed for the entrance. A familiar voice called, "Moonheart!" Blaze was running towards her calling, "Wait up!" "Blaze, you can't come with me. I'm on a mission." Blaze's tongue lolled out of his mouth. "I love secret missions! Please let me come. I may not be a Roamer yet, but that'll prepare me."

Graycloud and a white-furred dog named Skystar began to approach them. Moonheart began to panic. *If I tell them what I'm doing, will they let me go? Or will they lecture me on responsibility?*

Skystar was the first to speak. "What are you up to, Moon? Oh, wait! I forgot! You're supposed to be a Roamer now. I apologize, I forgot. You just don't look like one." She yelped as Graycloud stomped on her tail.

"What she means is that it is an honor to have you as a full-grown Roamer in the pack." "Whatever," Skystar mumbled, rolling her eyes. "Anyway," Graycloud continued, ignoring her, "where are you two off to this late? It's almost dinner time." Moonheart glared at Blaze, who took three steps away from her. She had to find a way to stall them so she could leave the camp.

"We were about to go hunting. I saw the prey pile earlier and, well, I don't think it's enough to feed our pack and the wolf pack."

Graycloud nodded in understanding and walked away. Skystar huffed, then followed him. "You almost blew my cover!" Moonheart quietly growled to Blaze. "It won't be a secret mission if we get caught before we even get to start!" She turned back toward the entrance and dashed out of the camp.

The sun had begun to set as they entered Stormpack's territory. Moonheart and Blaze had caught four plump squirrels and two water voles. The scent of the wolves still lingered around the forest, but it was stale.

Moonheart wove around trees, jumped over several logs, and crawled through some bramble bushes until they finally reached the camp. "Maybe we could steal some of their prey," Blaze said, licking his lips. Moonheart shook her head. "Then we would be in some big trouble. How do you think we'll explain to the wolves why their pile is empty?"

Blaze shrugged and they walked into the camp, their flanks barely touching. The camp had withered shrubs here and there and a lone tree stood tall out of the ground. "Wait, I forgot to ask, why are we here anyway?" Moonheart ignored the question and walked towards a den with vines hanging down from it. A pile of bones sat outside of it. Blaze's ear twitched and he crouched down, growling. Moonheart too heard a

sound, a scraping kind of noise. Coming from the pile
of bones.

CHAPTER 7

Moonheart could smell Blaze's fear coming off his bristling fur. Bravely and very quietly, she moved toward the pile. She removed the bones one by one, jumping at every clattering sound. Finally, a hole was revealed. A deep hole that looked never-ending

Moonheart looked over her shoulder at Blaze, who was shivering. Under the fear of revealing the pile, she hadn't even noticed how cold it was here. A gust of wind ruffled her gray fur, and she shook her whole body. Luckily, the hole was sloped. They could walk down into the darkness. "Wait, Moonheart, I don't know if we should do this. Who knows what could be down there and..." He trailed off, staring into space. "If you don't want to come with me, then you can guard the entrance. I must know what's down here."

With a final shake, she descended into the dark hole. The ground was damp and rocky. She almost slipped a couple of times, but soon found leverage in crevices. The tunnel leveled out onto flat terrain. There was a sudden howl that made Moonheart's fur prickle. Her paws tingled with nervous excitement as she journeyed on.

The scraping continued to ring in her ears, but there was no scent, which made her fur stand on end. The tunnel opened out into a cave. A scrawny body was silhouetted by moonlight spilling in from a hole in the ceiling. The scraping and howling were louder in here, and it was coming from the silhouette. "Hello?" She whimpered quietly. The scraping and howling stopped suddenly and the silhouette whipped its head around. "Who goes there!" It called out. "My name is Moonheart, I don't want to hurt you. But I will if I must.

There were five heartbeats of silence and then a whimper. "It's nice to finally have company down here." There was another long pause before the voice came again. "Moonheart. A beautiful name. I knew you were out there somewhere." Moonheart flicked her tail in confusion. Surely this old dog didn't know her, did she?

"The last time I saw you was seasons ago. You were so small and defenseless. I missed you so much. I knew one day I would see you again." Moonheart seemed taken aback. What was going on? This dog seemed to know Moonheart, but she didn't know her.

"Who are you?" Moonheart asked. There was a tense silence, and then finally she responded, "My name is Silverstone, your mother." Moonheart stood there, staring into the darkness. She couldn't even think straight. This old dog was her mother. She had been living here all this time.

"But— my mother— she died a long time ago. There is no way you could be my mother!" Silverstone slowly rose to her paws and walked over to Moonheart. Flashbacks of the dream she had in her last battle, when the strange dog from her dream had approached her. This was exactly what it was trying to warn her about. The dog from her dream...was Silverstone.

"I know it's hard to believe," she continued, "but I had to give you away so long ago. It was for your safety." Silverstone touched noses with Moonheart and then sat down in front of her. "I know it's been so long, but I can fix this. I know I can. We can go hunting together, or maybe you can show me how my pack is doing."

Moonheart's ears pricked up at that. "What do you mean, your pack?" Silverstone chuckled. "Before I was imprisoned, I used to be the alpha of a pack. But I gave those responsibilities up to someone else. What was her name again?" Silverstone looked down at her paws, thinking. "Oh yes! Now I remember. Her name was Sunnystorm. She was so loyal to my pack. Probably the most loyal dog I've ever known in my whole life."

Moonheart couldn't speak. Sunnystorm had never said anything about who her mother was, or who the Alpha was before her. It was heartbreaking.

Moonheart staggered back a step. "You abandoned me? You left me for someone else? What kind of mother are you?" Before she could answer, Blaze came tumbling out of the tunnel. "Moonheart! The wolves are back!"

CHAPTER 8

Moonheart and Blaze clawed their way back up to the surface. Silverstone had followed them, but she had stayed silent. The camp was the same as they got to the top, but the smell of many wolves was carried by the wind.

"We have to get out of here," Moonheart told them. Blaze and Silverstone both nodded. They began searching every inch of the camp for an escape route but found none. By then she could hear the pounding of paws coming closer and closer to the camp.

"Over here!" Silverstone shouted suddenly. She led them to a small den draped with lichen. The stench of rotten prey filled her nostrils. Blaze's eyes grew wide. "How could they live with this stench in the camp?" Silverstone growled. "They use it to teach recruits how to be brave. It's a foolish trick, scaring pups into being brave."

Silverstone walked into the den with Moonheart and Blaze following more slowly. The acrid scent filled the whole den. "In here," Silverstone whispered. Moonheart was surprised by the commanding tone in her voice. But she was a former Alpha, so that would make sense.

Silverstone uncovered a hole big enough for two dogs to fit into. "Go!" She barked as the smell overwhelmed Blaze and Moonheart. Blaze settled down on one side of the hole. Moonheart turned to look at her mother. "But what about you?"

Silverstone sighed and licked Moonheart on the head. "Stay here until I come back." Silverstone stared into Moonheart's blue eyes and carefully said, "I promise you; I will come back."

She nudged Moonheart into the hole and covered them with the rotten prey. Darkness engulfed the two dogs and they lay there, shaking with fear.

It seemed like moons before Moonheart watched the prey being removed from on top of them. Silverstone was grooming her fur while she waited for the two young dogs to exit the hole.

When Moonheart emerged, Silverstone walked over to her and groomed hers too. She did the same with Blaze. "The wolves have left," she reported, "but I don't know where they have gone. I followed the scent trail through the forest but then I lost it and came back to you two. Who knows how long they'll be gone; we need to get out of here as soon as possible."

She dashed out of the den and out of the camp with Moonheart and Blaze following. On their way back to camp they picked up all the prey they had caught earlier and carried them back to the camp. When they entered, they dropped their catch in the prey pile and ran straight for the den, ignoring the many questioning stares everyone gave them.

When they entered the den, Sunnystorm was sitting down in her moss bed with her head hanging down. Moonheart fixed her gaze on what she was looking at and stifled a gasp. There, sprawled out in front of Sunnystorm, was Fangtooth.

CHAPTER 9

Sunnystorm whipped her head around at the sound. When her eyes landed on Silverstone, she looked like her heart had skipped a beat. "Wha— but how did—" She could not seem to get words out. Silverstone strode over to Sunnystorm. Moonheart could see the size difference between them. Silverstone was much bigger, and her coat had grown with age, making her seem even larger.

"You died! How are you here?" Silverstone rested her head on hers and Moonheart could see her whisper something in Sunnystorm's ear. A tear ran down Sunnystorm's cheek and hit the floor of the den.

Moonheart turned her gaze back to Fangtooth. Blaze had already settled himself beside his former Beta. He was whimpering sadly while smoothing out

Fangtooth's ruffled fur. Moonheart sat down beside him and touched his flank with hers to comfort him.

Silverstone said suddenly, "What has happened to Fangtooth?" Sunnystorm closed her eyes and crouched down next to him. "I found him here like this. Can you believe it? Someone did this to him."

Blaze sat up straight suddenly. "The wolves!" Silverstone's fur bristled. "The wolves are in my camp!?" "It's ok," Sunnystorm said, "they are not causing any trouble." "It is them!" Blaze objected. "Look! It has gray fur, and it reeks of their smell. I know it was them, Sunnystorm."

Sunnystorm stormed out of the den and the dogs scrambled after her. The wolves were finishing breakfast and they looked up as Sunnystorm approached them. When they saw Silverstone at her side, their faces turned to horror.

Stormfoot calmly walked out to greet them, daring to take a glance in Silverstone's direction. "Good morning, Sunnystorm. What do you need from us?" Sunnystorm's eyes were full of hatred. "I know what you did, and you will be punished for it." She growled. But

Stormfoot didn't seem threatened by this, so he stood firm, facing Sunnystorm with pure bravery.

"I do not know what you're talking about, but if we were accused of something we will find out who did it." Sunnystorm flattened her ears to her skull. "I know what you did, and you will pay for it."

The rest of the wolf pack surrounded their Alpha protectively. "Fine, you caught me, but at least I got some sweet revenge on him before I did," he growled.

"You did this on purpose!?" Blaze half growled half whimpered.

"Of course, young one. He caused a lot of trouble with my pack, and it was good for him to feel what my pack felt." He smiled an awfully happy smile, but it disappeared when he fixed his gaze on Silverstone.

"And you were imprisoned in our camp for declaring war between our kind," he paused, "and for refusing to make me the Alpha of your pack. Now your pack shall be punished for all their crimes." He flicked his tail and the wolves charged for the dogs. But Sunnystorm was prepared. She howled and dogs came flooding out of their dens.

Moonheart leaped on top of a brown-furred wolf and was able to pin them down, but another wolf rammed into her side, knocking her off the wolf.

Blaze was wrestling with a wolf twice his size. When he saw Moonheart, he gave the wolf one final bite and dashed over to help her. With their combined strength, they were able to drive the wolf out of the camp.

"Thanks," panted Moonheart. Blaze gave a quick nod and ran back into the battle. Silverstone was fighting three wolves at a time, and she seemed to be winning. The three wolves had the size of a Recruit and stood no chance against Silverstone. They dashed out of the camp whimpering helplessly.

The dogs seemed to be winning against the wolves. But Moonheart's triumph didn't last long. When she looked across the clearing, she saw that Stormfoot had pinned Sunnystorm to the ground. As quickly as she could, Moonheart dashed over to help her. She rammed into Stormfoot's side knocking him off Sunnystorm. Moonheart scrambled to Sunnystorm's side and helped her to her paws.

Stormfoot was slowly getting up, chuckling as he did. "I guess it's time I put my second plan into motion."

He did an ear-splitting howl that filled the forest and the wolves that had retreated out of the camp came back. But they were now holding flaming sticks.

51

CHAPTER 10

The wolves threw the sticks all around the camp, setting it ablaze. Stormfoot managed to sneak off while they were distracted by the roaring fire that filled the camp. The wolf pack scrambled out of the entrance tunnel and back into the forest while the dogs panicked.

"Everyone, call down!" That was Sunnystorm, leaping on top of a large boulder. "Head for the edge of the territory towards the river. I will give more instructions once we get there."

She jumped off the boulder and bounded toward the entrance with the rest of the pack hard on her heels. Moonheart began to follow when she heard a squeal coming from one of the dens. A black pup was at the entrance to the nursery den and was shaking with fear as she stared in horror at the burning camp.

Moonheart jumped over a burning log and picked up the pup by its scruff. Just as she was about to dash toward the entrance tunnel, a branch fell from an oak and landed in front of the den. They were trapped.

Dropping the pup, she began to dig under the branch. Smoke spilled into the den, making it harder to breathe. "Hold on, I'm coming, Moonheart!" The familiar voice of Silverstone was outside the wall of fire. A moment later, she leaped through the fire. When she landed, her fur was blackened by the fire, and she was wheezing pitifully. She first grabbed the pup and leaped back through the fire. After a moment passed, she came back and picked Moonheart up by the scruff of her neck. She jumped through the fire and dropped Moonheart next to the yelping pup. There was a cracking noise coming from the great oak. Looking up, Silverstone quickly knocked Moonheart back. The burning branch fell straight on top of Silverstone, and she lay motionless.

"Mother!" Moonheart cried out. She stared in shock for a while longer before picking up the small pup and carrying her out of the camp, knowing that was what Silverstone would have told her to do. Taking a final glance back at her burning home, she dashed toward the river.

When Moonheart arrived at the river, a black female dog named Nightriver dashed toward the pup. "Hazel! I was worried sick, are you ok? Are you hurt?" She began licking Hazel all over, cleaning the ashes off her.

Sunnystorm approached her with a look of worry spread across her face. "I can't find Silverstone, have you seen her?" Moonheart lowered her head, flashbacks of the moment her mother was crushed by the burning tree branch. "I'm sorry, Sunnystorm, but she's gone." Blaze trotted next to Moonheart and pressed his flank against hers.

The rest of the pack were murmuring worriedly among each other. Moonheart gazed into the forest beyond the river. "Sunnystorm," she said in a voice barely a whisper, "what if we traveled farther beyond our territory? There might be a refuge somewhere out there."

Sunnystorm nodded her agreement and signaled with her tail for her pack to follow her across the river. As they entered the unfamiliar territory, Moonheart could hear the distant roar of cars. Winter made this part of the forest look eerily creepy. Moonheart could smell the fear scent coming off the rest of the pack. She too was afraid to enter this region.

Human dens spread far and wide in many directions. There weren't many prey scents around this part of the forest and Moonheart's belly growled hungrily. There was a rustling sound in the bushes ahead of them and the dogs stopped immediately. A small, white, short-haired dog emerged from the bushes. This was a den dog, a human's pet.

"Hello, fellow dogs!" She said. "My name is Cloe and I'd welcome you to my part of the forest, but the thing is, you're not welcome." There was a whistling sound that interrupted Cloe and three young humans came crashing through the trees. They took one look at the pack of dogs and made a loud, yelping noise. Two bigger humans came through the trees, looked at the other dogs, and then dashed to catch them. "Run!" Sunnystorm shouted. Ruby had begun to run but was caught by a human. Skystar stood her ground, growling and slashing at the humans. But she too was captured. Caught off guard, Moonheart herself was lifted into the air and carried back into the forest toward the human's dens.

The humans squeaked happily while they journeyed through the forest toward their dens. When they reached it, they were put down on a lush green carpet. "Ugh! I can't believe I'm being held captive with you!" Skystar spat at Moonheart. "Well, maybe if you hadn't been stomping and talking all loudly, maybe we wouldn't be here!" Moonheart retorted.

Cloe strode up to them wearing a smug expression. "Well, welcome to my home. I hope you enjoy it; you'll be here for a while." She laughed and walked into the kitchen.

Ruby snorted and curled up in a sleeping circle. Skystar did the same, making sure she was far enough away from Moonheart. Thoughts of the recent events flooded into her mind. The murder of Fangtooth, the death of her mother, and the fire that now raged through their home. Why was this happening? As Moonheart turned her sleep circles, she turned this thought over in her mind. Why is this happening to *me?* The scent of Silverstone filled her nostrils and Moonheart almost thought that she could see her sitting in front of her, watching over her. Unexpectedly, she took a huge yawn, closed her eyes, and let sleep engulf her.

CHAPTER 11

Four moons had passed since they had been captured by the humans. At that time, they discovered that these humans also had a cat.

"Oh great, it's bad enough that I have to live with you, but now I have to live with that disgraceful thing?" Skystar had sneered.

Nobody had come to rescue them. They had to survive the taunting of Cloe, the slop the humans fed them, and the constant noise the humans made.

Now it was night and Moonheart could not sleep. Cloe snored lightly while Skystar growled in her sleep a few times. Mittens, the ginger tom, slept on top of a cat tree. "It's not fair that they get more comfy bedding than we do!" Ruby had complained, taking after her trainer, Skystar.

As Moonheart watched the sun fade into the distance and the moon rise, there was a scraping noise coming from the small doggy door at the back of the room. Curious, she got up and sniffed around. Detecting a familiar scent, she whispered, "Thornstripe? What are you doing here?" There was silence before another voice whispered, "I'm here, too!" The unexpected scent of Blaze startled her, and she had to shake herself before continuing. "It's good to hear you too, Blaze. how are—"

"It's Blazefang, now. Named after Fangtooth," He interrupted. Disappointed to miss his Roamer Ceremony, she continued, "Are you here to rescue us? Because we could use the help. I'll go wake the others." There was a snort of impatience that Moonheart guessed came from Thornstripe.

Excitedly, she ran to Skystar and began to nudge her. "What do you want, pup? Can't a dog get any sleep around here?" Quickly and quietly, she explained to her how Thornstripe and Blazefang were here to rescue them. "About time," Skystar said as Moonheart finished. "This bed is making my joints ache!"

While Skystar prepared herself to leave, Moonheart explained to Ruby, who had the same reaction as Skystar when awakened. Without speaking, Ruby nodded and prepared herself to leave.

Moonheart was about to turn to the doggy door when a hissing startled her. "Well, what's this about an escape?" It was Mittens, who stared through slitted eyes. "Not on my watch." Mittens caterwauled so loud, that Moonheart thought that the whole neighborhood would wake.

A few heartbeats later a human came crashing through the door. "Come on, let's go!" Thornstripe shouted, poking her head through the doggy door. Skystar was the first to dash through it, followed by Ruby and Moonheart.

The fresh cold breeze hit her like a bolt of lightning. "Follow me to the new camp," called Thornstripe over her shoulder as she went through a gaping hole in the ground that led under the wooden fence.

It took a while for the dogs to reach the new Breezepack camp. As dawn stretched across the sky, a new unfamiliar scent filled the air.

Blazefang and Thornstripe led them into a small ravine where dogs were carrying out their daily tasks. Sunnystorm lay basking in front of a cleft in a rock. Her ear twitched, warning her of their presence. Noticing Moonheart she leaped to her paws. "It is good to see you. All of you," she added quickly, glancing in Skystar's direction.

"Excuse me, Sunnystorm!" This was Nightriver calling, bounding over to them, flanked by Hazel. "Yes, Nightriver?"

"I wanted to know, Hazel has grown, and I think she's ready to become a Recruit. If it's okay with you."

Sunnystorm took a good look at Hazel, who shrunk back behind her mother's leg. "Yes, I will have her ceremony at once." Flicking her tail to dismiss the group of dogs, she bounded on top of a boulder that overlooked the camp. "Dogs of Breezepack, gather here for a meeting!" She shouted. Moonheart hadn't even noticed the many dens spread out around the camp.

As the dogs started to settle down in front of the boulder, Sunnystorm beckoned for Hazel to step up. "Hazel, I see that it is time for you to play your part in the pack and to fulfill your destiny as a Recruit. Are you ready?" Shakily, Hazel nodded. "Then, with the power vested in me, I pronounce you as a Recruit!" Howls of congratulations broke out among the camp. Signaling with her tail for silence, Sunnystorm continued. "Your trainer will be none other than Moonheart. I have heard of what she did to save you in the fire. She is a brave warrior and a talented fighter. I hope that she passes down everything she knows to you."

More howls broke out among the gathered pack and Moonheart felt pride swell up inside of her. Hazel walked over to sit beside Moonheart. She seemed just as excited as Moonheart felt. *My Recruit!* She thought. The pack surrounded them to congratulate them. Moonheart looked down at Hazel, who had closed her eyes, taking in the praise.

"We can't stay here too long," Moonheart whispered into her ear. "I'm sure we have a lot of prey to catch." Hazel looked into Moonheart's blue eyes. "Ok, Moonheart. I'm ready to go."

They slipped through the dogs toward the entrance tunnel, only stopping to talk to Nightriver. "You will be careful out there, won't you?" She asked. Hazel pressed her muzzle to hers. "Don't worry, danger will cower before me." Moonheart loved Hazel's enthusiasm. *I wonder if Silverstone would have done the same thing with me. Would she be just as worried as Nightriver?* She thought with a pang of loss.

With a final lick on the head, Nightriver let them pass. They stalked through the forest toward the river. Moonheart shivered as she saw the shriveled bushes and the ash that covered the ground. Hazel, Moonheart noticed, had shrunk back behind her, staring wide-eyed at the scene, probably having flashbacks.

The scent of bandicoot filled her nostrils, and she glanced down at Hazel. "Tell me, can you smell anything?" Hazel carefully sniffed the air. "Ash, humans, but it's very faint. And bandicoot!" She dashed off into the undergrowth, returning triumphantly with a bandicoot dangling from her jaws.

"Very impressive," Moonheart said. Hazel set it down in front of them. "Can we share it?" Her eyes were full of respect for Moonheart, and she felt sympathy. Laying down next to her, they began to devour the bandicoot together in famished bites.

The sun began to set behind the trees and Moonheart sighed. "I can feel that you will be a talented

Roamer. Keep training hard, and you might even be Alpha." Hazel looked down at her paws. "I don't know about Alpha, but I can still try my best." Hazel rested her head on her paws and sighed. Moonheart had to admit that Hazel did have potential in her. It just had to be brought out.

Resting her head on her paws, she looked across the river. For a moment, she thought that she could see her mother, Silverstone. But with a blink, she was gone. Moonheart closed her eyes and drifted off to sleep, the warmness of Hazel's flank soothing her.

CHAPTER 12

The next day was normal. After waking up in the forest, Moonheart and Hazel caught a decent amount of prey. They had to hide from the humans a couple of times, but they didn't get caught.

That is until they bumped into Cloe and Mittens while heading back to camp. Cloe looked more confused than surprised, and Mittens showed pure hatred in his eyes.

"Where exactly do you think you're going?" He asked. "And who's your little friend?" Cloe approached Hazel but jumped back when she snapped at her. "We're just passing through," said Moonheart. Mittens chuckled. "After what you did, this is our territory now. And I believe you and your little dog pack are on it."

With a final hiss, Mittens launched himself at Moonheart.

Realizing the size difference between them, Moonheart swatted Mittens away. "We don't have time for this," she told Hazel as she swatted Cloe away as well.

Before they could recover, Moonheart and Hazel dashed off toward the camp. When they returned, the camp was just waking up. Sighing, Moonheart and Hazel each grabbed a piece of prey and ate by the boulder.

Hazel stopped abruptly as Skystar approached with Ruby close behind. "Hey, you two! Sunnystorm wants us to patrol the territory, and make sure there are no wolves here." She looked down directly at Moonheart. "Of course, you might not want to hurt your kind, so I guess you could stay behind." Skystar and Ruby retreated to the tunnel, laughing the whole way

+++

The four dogs had spent the rest of the day patrolling the territory, only stopping to catch dinner. Ruby yawned. "Why do we have to do this with them?" She complained to Skystar, flicking her tail in Moonheart and Hazel's direction.

"Because it was Sunnystorm's orders. If it wasn't, then we'd be done patrolling by now." Skystar shot daggers at Moonheart, and she returned it with a low growl. Hazel, however, was eating her squirrel peacefully, not minding the insults Skystar and Ruby sent at her.

"I think it's time we're leaving anyway," Moonheart said, getting up. The dogs ventured back toward the camp. When they reached it, Skystar and Moonheart had been in an argument about whose Recruit was stronger. She turned to ask Hazel to show Skystar how much she had learned but discovered that neither Hazel or Ruby were there.

"Where'd they go?" Both Skystar and Moonheart said in unison. Worriedly, they dashed back out of the camp. It didn't take long for them to catch their scent. What made Moonheart nervous was how the scent led to the river. On the opposite side of the bank, two sets of paw tracks were leading deeper into their old territory.

"Those fur-brains!" Muttered Skystar. Moonheart's heart stopped dead when a yowling came from their old territory. Without thinking, she leaped into the water. It bared the chill of winter as it lapped at her fur. When she reached the bank, she dashed through the forest toward the yowling. Shrubs from the fire pulled at her long fur but she didn't stop.

She began to scent Hazel and Ruby, but it was mingled with the tang of blood and wolves. When she reached the scene, her heart skipped two whole beats. Laying in front of her was the lifeless body of Ruby. Skystar ran out of the bushes behind her and stopped dead, paralyzed on the spot. "No..." She whispered.

Moonheart's eyes flickered to where Hazel was beginning to get up. Moonheart stifled a gasp. Hazel's right eye had a claw mark that stretched down to her muzzle. But it was not the scar that made her gasp. It was the blank eye.

Moonheart's eyes traveled down to Hazel's hind leg. It was bleeding so heavily that she was surprised that she could still move it a little bit. "M— Moonheart." She said in a croaky voice. "I— I'm so sorry. I di— didn't want to c— come over here. B— but Ruby persuaded me to." Hazel began to tip over, but Moonheart caught her just in time. "Don't waste your breath. Bluepetal will fix you up, don't worry. It's going to be ok."

Skystar sadly picked up Ruby and together they took their Recruits back to camp silently.

+++

When Moonheart and Skystar finally reached the camp, it didn't take long for news about Ruby's death and Hazel's injuries to spread. Nightriver groomed Hazel's ruffled fur thoroughly while whispering words of comfort to her. Bluepetal dashed out of her den as soon as she heard about the injured Hazel. When she finished inspecting her, she said to Nightriver, "I'm sorry, but I'm afraid all I can do is give her some ginger to take away the pain and some valerian roots so she can get some rest. The leg will have to heal on its own. I'll wrap some vines around the leg to stop her from moving it."

Bluepetal herded Hazel to her den and murmurs quickly broke out among the camp. Sunnystorm stepped out of her den and howled to silence the anxious dogs. She bounded to the top of the Meeting Boulder, but did not have to call the dogs, for they were already anxiously waiting for what Sunnystorm had to say.

"Dogs of BreezePack, as we all know, our oldest Recruit Ruby has been killed and our youngest Hazel has been injured. She will live another day, but we grieve for Ruby. She was a strong and talented dog and would have made a great Roamer one day."

There was a moment's pause before she continued. "Meanwhile, we will continue the tradition of the pack. It has been a long while since we've had a Beta, and it is time for me to appoint a new one." She gazed among all the dogs. Seeing if the dog she chose was there, Moonheart guessed. "I give the role of Beta to none other than Graycloud. He has proven his loyalty countless times, and we honor him for that."

The dogs in the clearing barked happily as Graycloud made his way towards the boulder. With a flick of her tail, Sunnystorm ended the meeting and she and Graycloud went to their den.

Moonheart found her paws taking her to Bluepetal's den. When she stepped inside, sweet smells filled her nostrils, and she began to feel dizzy. Inside the cave, Bluepetal was whispering something into Hazel's ear.

Finally, Bluepetal noticed Moonheart's presence and beckoned her over. She spoke in a soft, quiet voice. "I've already talked this over with Sunnystorm and Hazel herself, but I need your approval." Moonheart pricked her ears up to show that she was giving her her attention. "Well," she continued, "Hazel's injuries show that she may not be able to finish her training. She would have to always stay in camp unless it was necessary to leave. But... I've thought of another way she could impact the pack." Bluepetal took a deep breath and looked Moonheart right in the eye. "But I need your approval first." Moonheart nodded. "I was thinking, maybe Hazel could be my Recruit?"

C H A P T E R   1 3

Moonheart stared blankly at the cave wall for a moment. *If I say yes, then I might be helping Hazel. It'll show her there are more ways to help the pack than being a Roamer. But then I'd lose her...* "Oh, please Moonheart." Hazel was now in a sitting position, staring at Moonheart with a begging yellow eye. Moonheart sighed and nodded. "Of course, she can. If it means she still can help the pack in some way, then of course."

Hazel leaped to her paws and began chasing her tail around in circles excitedly. Moonheart felt a thorn stab her heart when she realized that this lively Recruit used to be hers.

Just then, there was a rustling in the grasses that covered the entrance and Thornstripe emerged through it. "What's up with her?" Thornstripe asked as she glanced at Hazel. "She looks as if she was just made Alpha." Bluepetal gave a quick summary of what she told Moonheart.

Thornstripe looked at Moonheart and, for the first time in moons, smiled. "You have grown fond of this Recruit, haven't you?"

There was another rustle in the grass and Blazefang emerged from the entrance. "There you are, Moonheart! I've been looking all over camp for you. I was going to ask if you wanted to go hunting." Blazefang, Moonheart noticed, was nervously scraping the earth with his forepaw. "Of course I will. I need to shake some things off my mind anyway." And together, they walked out of the camp.

+++

Moonheart was only a few inches away from the squirrel she had been tracking. Her scent was downwind, and she was so close to the ground she would probably make a whole ditch. She bunched up her muscles, ready to jump, when all of a sudden, a flash of red streaked across the ground and killed the squirrel with a swift bite.

"Show off," Moonheart murmured as Blazefang picked up the squirrel. The sun was setting in a ball of fire, turning the tops of the trees to flame and sending long shadows across the forest floor. Moonheart shivered as flashbacks of the recent fire flooded into her brain. She was about to follow Blazefang back to the camp when a blue light caught her eye.

Following it, it led her toward the river that bordered the wolves' territory and the dogs' new territory. There, on the other side of the river, sat Silverstone. Her fur was glowing as if she were made of pure stars. "Greetings, my daughter." She said coolly. "I see that you have been having problems ever since my absence.

Moonheart was too awestruck to speak. Her mother was talking to her, right now! It was only Blazefang's call that brought her back to reality. She looked across the river to see that Silverstone was now gone. Heaving a sigh, she went on with the thought that she was tired and seeing things. When they returned to camp, everything was quiet. All but the yapping of pups. *Pups!?* Moonheart thought suddenly. Panic-stricken, she ran toward the source of the sound. She entered a wide-open den with a pool of water centering it. There, in the corner of the den, lay Winterpelt with two small pups. Winterpelt looked up at Moonheart warmly. "Surprise!" She said in a weak voice. Boltwing trotted into the den carrying sticks and moss. His face showed he was very proud.

"But— You never—" Moonheart struggled to find the right words. "We wanted to keep it a surprise for you. I felt it ever since we went on patrol with you. And now they're here! Frost and Speck!" Moonheart felt her tail tingling as it started to wag. "Those are beautiful names, Winterpelt. Look at Frost! She has your blue eyes and a whitish-gray coat. And Speck has the amber eyes and the orange fur and black splotches on her pelt like Boltwing, except that she has white paws."

Boltwing beamed at the praise and laid down next to Winterpelt, watching the pups in a playful scuffle. A scraping at the entrance alerted them to a new presence. Hazel limped into the den carrying a raspberry leaf. "Here." she said, dropping it in front of Winterpelt. "It's useful to have after you give birth."

Moonheart smiled at her former Recruit. She seemed to already be taking her new responsibilities very seriously. Telling Winterpelt goodbye, she and

Blazefang backed out of the den and went toward the Roamers' den. "Finally," Blazefang said when they were out of earshot, "we can live in peace without wolves bothering us with so-called peace treaties."

They reached the den and were greeted by complete silence. Skystar was already sleeping. She twitched constantly, though. Moonheart sighed at the thought that Graycloud no longer slept in this den. In the far corner lay Thornstripe who drew her tongue over her dusty pelt. Nightriver was sitting on her nest, staring up at the ceiling. Lastly, Talonfoot was pacing not far away from Skystar. With a jolt, she remembered that they were littermates. *He must be worried about Skystar.* She thought.

Waving to him with her tail, she settled down in her nest. She had hardly closed her eyes when Cometfire burst in through the gorse. "Did I forget to change anyone's bedding?" The small dog panted. Blazefang chuckled. "Nope, they're all very comfy. Thanks." That seemed to reassure him because then he walked over to his own nest and plopped down. In no time, his flank began to rise and fall in a peaceful slumber.

Blazefang shook his head in amusement. "That dog!" Then he too turned his sleep circles and began to snore lightly.

Finally, Moonheart could close her eyes. Her dreams were blurry and a little chaotic. Wolves rampaging into the camp, the sun shooting bursts of flame down into the forest, Moonheart flailing her legs in a flood until finally she was prodded awake. She began to blink the rest of her sleep from her eyes when she realized who had woken her.

"At last," Silverstone said triumphantly. "I can finally reach you!"

CHAPTER 14

"What are you doing here!?" Moonheart said, awestruck.

"I came to talk to you," Silverstone said calmly.

"But how?" Moonheart shot back.

Silverstone sighed heavily. "That is information I wouldn't dare tell. But, let me get to the point. You have a bright future ahead of you, Moonheart. Just wait and see." Moonheart looked down at her paws to see that water surrounded her. She looked wildly around to see that dogs were beginning to approach her.

They formed a circle around Moonheart. The surrounding dogs bowed their heads and Moonheart felt the water rising, filling the whole den until she could no longer see. Moonheart shot her eyes open. She looked around. Skystar was the only one still in the den, grooming her fur. "No dog can get any sleep around here with you doing all that yelping and scratching." She growled. The den was not engulfed in water and there were no dogs bowing to her and there was certainly no way that her mother was talking to her.

Shaking the last scraps of moss off her, she left the den. The sun was shining brightly above the camp. Frost and Speck were outside playing with the colorful leaves on the ground, Winterpelt watching them with pure love in her eyes. Speck spotted Moonheart and dashed over. Frost followed her sister excitedly. "Hi Moonheart!" Said Speck. "I'm ready for training!" Moonheart couldn't help but laugh. "Not yet! You're not old enough for that." "I want you as my trainer!" Said Frost, wagging her tail. "No, she's mine!" Speck shot back. They then got into a friendly fight, rolling over and swatting small paws at each other.

Winterpelt came to join her, chuckling. "These pups! They are such rascals." Just then, Graycloud emerged from the entrance tunnel with Talonfoot, Blazefang, and Nightriver following. They had small mice and scrawny squirrels dangling from their jaws. They dropped the pitiful catch into the pile and began to separate.

Moonheart then realized how hungry she was and decided to pick a squirrel from the pile. It was stringy but she didn't care, Moonheart felt like she could eat a whole human den.

Blazefang walked over to join her, his tail dragging in the sand. Talonfoot followed more slowly behind. "You guys look terrible," Moonheart commented. "I know! Blazefang said. "Graycloud was so terrible. He made us *run* the whole patrol. And then he told us to try and catch a deer. A *deer* Moonheart! By ourselves! In the middle of winter!" Moonheart was surprised at his tone of voice. After all, he used to be Graycloud's Recruit.

"What have you been doing this morning?" Ask Talonfoot. He seemed relaxed now that he was talking to someone. "Not much, I just got up. But last night—" Moonheart stopped. How could she tell them what had happened last night? Would they believe her? "Last night, I think I ate too much. I had crazy dreams. But let's not get into details."

From the other side of the clearing, Graycloud was approaching them. "Oh no..." Groaned Blazefang. "I wanted to tell you what a nice job you both did while hunting today. We may not have caught that deer, but we caught plenty of other things. We'll get 'em next time!" "Next time?" Blazefang growled. Before leaving, Graycloud turned to Moonheart to say, "and Sunnystorm wants to see you in her den," and then walked off to talk with Winterpelt.

Moonheart said bye to her friends and walked to Sunnystorm's den. She stood in the cleft in the rock and called into the darkness. "Enter," said Sunnystorm's voice. Moonheart walked down the tunnel into a wide-open clearing. Sunnystorm lay in the center, staring into space. At first, Moonheart thought she might be dead. Then, she saw the normal rise and fall of her flank.

"You wanted to see me?" Moonheart asked. Sunnystorm rested her gaze on Moonheart. "I did. Moonheart, I haven't told anyone this yet, so do you promise to keep this secret?" Moonheart flicked her ears with embarrassment. "What secret? And why are you choosing to tell me, over your own Beta?" Sunnystorm shook her head. "You, Moonheart, are the only one I trust. Graycloud, he wouldn't understand. I've already talked it over with Bluepetal, though. She almost exploded with excitement. Have I ever told you that she was my sister?" Moonheart shook her head vigorously. She could see the resemblance in their brown coats. The only difference is that Sunnystorm had green eyes and Bluepetal had blue ones.

"Anyway," she continued, "what I'm about to tell you is very important to the pack." Moonheart listened nervously, her fur prickling. "Moonheart, as you know, Fangtooth was my Beta before Graycloud. But what you don't know is how I'm having our pup, according to Bluepetal, in about two moons." This information hit Moonheart like a gust of wind, making her stagger backward a step. "What? How long have you known?" Sunnystorm sighed. "For a while now. But when Fangtooth..." She paused and took a breath. "When he had his accident, I didn't know what to do. I panicked. I wasn't ready to care for her on my own."

Moonheart looked at her. Now that she thought about it, her belly did seem a little swollen. "What are you going to do about it?" Asked Moonheart curiously. Sunnystorm stood up on wobbly legs. At the same time, Bluepetal rushed into the den carrying a bundle of herbs. "Moonheart, I'll need you to leave, please." Moonheart took one final glance at Sunnystorm and slowly left the den. Thornstripe was waiting at the entrance. "What's going on? Why does Bluepetal keep going in there?" Moonheart shook her head. "I promised to keep it secret."

Thornstripe looked angry for a split second before nodding. Talonfoot sat alone by the camp entrance, staring at Moonheart and Thornstripe. Meeting Moonheart's eyes, he quickly looked away. Saying a quick goodbye to Thornstripe, who walked over to the fresh meat pile, she dashed over to him.

"Hi, Talonfoot. Are you on guard duty or what?" He nodded his head. "I just don't know what to do so I put myself on guard, watching the camp."

I nodded. "That's good. I was wondering if you could come with me to patrol the border. Thornstripe could come too. She must be dying to leave the camp." All right, it's a deal," he said, jumping up. "I'll go fetch her." And he ran off to the Roamer's den.

+++

As they approached the river, Moonheart could smell the fresh scent of wolves. "They must have been patrolling today," Thornstripe pointed out. Talonfoot sniffed the air and nodded. "I smell it too."

Moonheart shifted nervously on her paws. She wanted to go back to her real home. She wanted to know what the wolves had changed in the forest.

Waiting for Thornstripe and Talonfoot's backs to be turned, she quickly waded through the water. The scent of ash filled her nostrils, and she shivered as flashbacks of the fire entered her mind.

There was movement in one of the shriveled bushes and she growled instinctively. A bushy gray body emerged from it, her fangs glinting in the sunlight. "Well, if it isn't the half-breed." She said sneeringly. "I'll make sure you find your way off our territory. But not without some scars to remember."

She bunched her hind muscles and prepared to leap. But before she could, Thornstripe came bursting out of the bushes behind Moonheart, tackling the wolf.

They grappled on the ground until Talonfoot came running through the bushes. Startled, the wolf jumped up and ran in the direction of the wolf camp. "No doubt she'll be telling Stormfoot." Growled Thornstripe. Then she whipped around to Moonheart. "And what were you thinking, pup? Going onto wolf territory, are you mad?" Moonheart shrank back. "I was just curious. I wanted to see how the camp was doing. Or if it was maybe safe to come back?"

At once Moonheart regretted saying this. Thornstripe glared at her furiously. Then she turned around without another word and headed back toward the river. Moonheart looked hopefully at Talonfoot, but he just looked down at his paws, muttered "sorry," and followed Thornstripe.

Moonheart looked down at her paws. "I didn't mean to," she muttered. "I was just curious."

Her ears pricked up when there was another rustle in the bush. "I know, I know, I'm coming Thornstripe." She said, but as she was beginning to walk through the bushes, she ran into a red-haired dog whom she immediately recognized.

"Blazefang!? What are you doing here?" Blazefang looked down at Moonheart, utterly surprised. Then, a bushy-haired gray dog followed him out from the bushes. Moonheart's fur bristled. It was the same wolf that had just attacked them only moments ago. "*You!*" Growled Moonheart and the wolf in unison.

Moonheart crouched down, prepared to protect her friend, when Blazefang stood in front of her. "Moonheart, let me explain! This is Mistwhisper. She rescued me when I was trapped under some rocks that a cowardly squirrel led me into. Then I heard you talking to yourself again and I came to see what was up." Moonheart didn't look at Blazefang. She couldn't believe that he was standing next to a wolf. "Moonheart!" Thornstripe's voice rang out across the forest. Moonheart glared at the wolf. "Please don't tell anyone," Blazefang pleaded.

Moonheart pushed past Blazefang and headed toward the river without a final glance.

+++

The camp was silent when they got back. Blazefang hadn't made it back to the camp yet because when she entered the Roamer's den it was empty except for Skystar who was currently grooming her fur.

"How was patrol?" She asked without looking up. Moonheart was completely taken aback. Skystar had just said a complete sentence without teasing her about her wolf heritage. "It was—" Moonheart paused for a while. She wanted to tell Blazefang off for being caught with a wolf. But a feeling deep inside her stopped her from doing it.

"It was good. No wolves on the border." She said simply. Skystar nodded. "That's good." She groomed her fur for a little while longer before curling up and falling into a deep sleep. Moonheart began to do the same after being brought a juicy squirrel by Cometfire.

There was a rustling in the den entrance and Blazefang emerged. "Late, are you?" Growled Moonheart. Blazefang stopped immediately. "Moonheart, let it go, will you?" He growled back.

"No!" She was standing now. "After you become friends with a wolf you tell me to let it go?" "I'm friends with you, aren't I?" He shouted. Moonheart's fur was bristling angrily. "Or maybe I'm not," he muttered. He pushed back through the ferns and into the camp.

CHAPTER 15

Moonheart dashed out of the den. Blazefang's red tail was disappearing through the entrance tunnel. "Blazefang, wait!" Moonheart shouted desperately.

"Hey! Moonheart! You'll wake up the whole camp with your barking!" Moonheart whipped around to see Graycloud walking out of his den. "What's with the noise?"

Moonheart explained everything to him. How she ran into Blazefang and Mistwhisper. About their argument in the den and how he stormed out of the camp.

As she finally finished the story Graycloud was already making a beeline for the entrance. Instinctively, she followed. A cold breeze ruffled her fur, and the sky threatened a lot of snow. Blazefang sat alone at the edge of the river, his head down. Graycloud nodded to Moonheart, and she walked over to him sitting down beside him. "Look, Blazefang, I'm sorry. For everything." Blazefang remained silent. "I didn't mean what I said." More silence greeted Moonheart. She took a breath and looked into the water. Reflected on the surface was Silverstone. She nodded her head and smiled. *Let it go,* said an echoing voice in her head.

Sighing, Moonheart said, "Blazefang, if it makes you happy, I think you should go meet her." Blazefang's ears pricked up and he looked over at Moonheart. "But that means I won't be able to see you anymore." Moonheart licked Blazefang on the ear. "I won't forget you. After all, you are the pack's biggest troublemaker so it'll be hard to forget you." Blazefang laughed, stared deep into Moonheart's eyes, and dived into the river, crossing to the other side. With a final glance, he howled and Moonheart joined him. Then, he ran back through the forest, deeper into wolf territory.

+++

By the time they returned to camp, everyone was awake. Hazel emerged from the Healer's den. "I thought I heard you all shouting." Then she noticed Moonheart's glum face and asked, "Did something happen?" Thornstripe came out of the Roamer's den and joined the small group. Moonheart looked down at her paws, not wanting to meet Thornstripe's eyes.

"It's Blazefang, isn't it?" Hazel whispered. Sighing, Moonheart nodded. Hazel touched Moonheart's muzzle with her own comfortingly. Still, Moonheart didn't dare tell Blazefang's secret.

Sunnystorm came out of her den with Bluepetal close behind. "Where is he?" She growled. "Where is Blazefang?" Moonheart looked down at her paws. "He was attacked by a wolf," She lied. Sunnystorm glared down at Moonheart and for a second she thought she saw a smile. "Very well. We shall grieve for him. Get some rest. I will get Cometfire to bring you some prey."

Moonheart just realized how tired she felt. She headed for the den. When she entered, she was immediately tackled by two small dogs. "I got her!" Shouted Speck triumphantly. "No, I got her first!" Frost argued. "Get your paws off of her, she's mine, Frost!"

They got into a friendly argument on top of Moonheart. Not long after, Winterpelt entered the den.

"There you two are!" She exclaimed. "I've been searching the whole forest for you guys!" Her gaze traveled down to the bedraggled Moonheart. "And get off Moonheart! She needs to rest."

With a last little growl at each other, they followed their mother out of the den. As soon as they were out, Cometfire burst in through the entrance. "Is it true?" He panted. "Is he gone?" Moonheart nodded glumly. Cometfire's ears drooped and he dropped the squirrel he was carrying. "I'm so sorry Moonheart. I understand how close you two were." And without another word he dashed out of the den, howling the whole way.

"You've got everyone worried," said a startling voice. Looking behind her, the glowing outline of Silverstone sat in Blazefang's nest. Moonheart looked into her mother's eyes. "Was it you?" She asked. "Was it you who told me to let it go?" Silverstone nodded. "He would have gone anyway, despite what you told him."

Moonheart looked down at her paws. "What if something happens to him? What if he gets hurt or that wolf double-crosses him? I can't help him!"

"Moonheart," Silverstone said soothingly, "I will make sure he is safe. You need to calm down. He will be ok."

Talonfoot walked into the den. Moonheart blinked and Silverstone was gone. Talonfoot looked at Moonheart. "I'm so sorry," he muttered. Moonheart nodded. "He would have gone anyway, despite what I did," She recited her mother's words.

Talonfoot walked over and licked Moonheart on the head. Soon after, Hazel burst into the den. "Moonheart! Come quick! Sunnystorm needs you!" And she ran back out of the den.

Exchanging a worried glance with Talonfoot, she left the den. Anxious murmurs were being passed around the camp. Thornstripe sat at the entrance of Sunnystorm's den. "Do you know what's going on?" Moonheart asked her. "All I know is that Sunnystorm started howling and Bluepetal told me to stand guard so nobody could enter the den. She told Hazel to go fetch you."

Nodding to Thornstripe and taking in a gulp of air, she entered Sunnystorm's den. She was lying out on the ground, wheezing. Bluepetal was whispering something in her ear and Hazel was coming in and out of the den carrying a bundle of herbs.

Moonheart announced her arrival and Bluepetal called her over. "What's going on?" Said a panic-stricken Moonheart. "Don't worry, she'll be fine," Bluepetal whispered. "But what's going on!" Moonheart shouted and Bluepetal silenced her as Sunnystorm gave a final howl and then rested her head on her moss bedding.

A small squeak filled the den and understanding washed over Moonheart. She peeked over Bluepetal's shoulder to see a brownish-red pup lying on another smaller moss bed. Sunnystorm looked at her pup with love in her eyes. "Moonheart, what would you like to name her?"

Moonheart looked at Sunnystorm, surprised. She thought for a second before saying, "Rose. Her name is Rose." Sunnystorm and Bluepetal nodded. "Rose it is." Sunnystorm lay back down and, very quickly, fell asleep. "Could you stay with her and Rose tonight, Moonheart? Get me if anything happens." And with that, she left the den.

Moonheart looked down at the slumbering pup and her mother. There was a small glow at the back of the den that Moonheart immediately guessed was her mother before curling up, closing her eyes, and falling asleep

CHAPTER 16

The next few months were cold and tiring. Frost and Speck were growing up faster than ever. There was a day when the ground was covered in thick snow, and they almost snuck out of camp. Graycloud still sent the dogs out on hunting missions and border patrols, but Moonheart was glad to go so she could talk to Silverstone secretly.

Moonheart was coming back into camp carrying a fat vole. The days were becoming warmer. The camp was gathered around the Great Boulder, Sunnystorm on top of it.

Dropping her vole in the pile, she joined the pack as Sunnystorm said, "Frost, Speck, step up." The sisters exchanged excited glances at each other and walked up to the rock. "You have grown fast and are ready to become Recruits." She paused and gazed across the gathered dogs. "Frost, your Trainer shall be Skystar. After your loss of Ruby, I think you are ready to have another Recruit." There was a howl of approval around the camp and Frost headed toward Skystar. Sunnystorm waited for the noise to die down before continuing. "Speck, your Trainer shall be Moonheart. Hazel has moved on, and she is ready for a new Recruit." A chorus of howls followed her words as Speck headed towards Moonheart.

Sunnystorm ended the meeting with a flick of her tail and bounded to her den where Graycloud was waiting at the entrance. Speck was bouncing on her paws. "I see I'll have some trouble with you," Moonheart laughed. "Moonheart, for our first training lesson, I want to go to our old camp." Moonheart stared at her for a moment before responding. "This is our camp now. Our old camp is no longer ours." Speck only looked disappointed for a second.

After they had dinner, instead of heading to the den, Moonheart snuck out of camp and towards the river. Silverstone sat at the water's edge, staring at her reflection. "Mother?" Moonheart whispered. Silverstone turned her head around. It was either a trick of the light or it looked like she had tears in her eyes. "Moonheart, I'm afraid this will be the last time we meet. It is a danger to my secret and your life. As your mother and former pack Alpha, I command you to stop coming to see me."

Moonheart stood, awestruck. "But that'll mean I'll never see you again!" Silverstone chuckled. "Maybe, maybe not, only destiny knows." And with that, she faded away into the night.

The next day Moonheart took Speck out hunting. Again, they had to fight off Mittens and Cloe. They were walking down the camp entrance when there was a crash behind them. Moonheart and Speck whipped around just in time to see Blazefang running down the entrance tunnel looking bedraggled. "Moonheart! Gather the whole pack, you all need to leave now!"

Moonheart looked down at Speck and flicked her tail to Sunnystorm's den. Understanding, she ran off. "What's going on?" Moonheart asked once Speck was out of earshot. "The wolves, they're coming! They figured out I was back on their territory, and they chased me away. I heard them growl before I left, 'This is the last time those dogs will ever trespass on our territory,' and they ran back to their camp."

By the time Blazefang finished his story, Graycloud was already making his way toward them with Speck not far behind. Word that Blazefang was back got through the camp fast. Dogs were emerging from their dens and murmuring curiously. "Blazefang, explain to me what's going on."

As Blazefang retold his story, Moonheart thought she could hear howling in the distance. Speck was shaking with fear. "Moonheart?" She murmured. "Are wolves nice? My father told me about them and how they burned down our old camp and how they killed our old Beta." Moonheart looked deep into her eyes. They reminded her so much of Winterpelt.

"No," Moonheart said simply. "They are not nice, and I would advise you to go with the rest of the pack when we face them." Speck looked as if she was going to object but whether she did or not Moonheart didn't know, for she was now sprinting off towards Sunnystorm's den.

"Enter." Barked Sunnystorm's tired voice. Moonheart dashed inside. Sunnystorm was curled up around Rose who seemed to be trying very hard to pretend not to be awake, her twitching tail giving her away. "Sunnystorm, if Speck hasn't already told you—"

"Moonheart, we aren't going anywhere."

"What?" Moonheart said a little too loudly.

"You heard me right. We aren't moving."

Sunnystorm slowly got up from her bedding, making Rose jump up. "But— the wolves—"

"Are not going to chase us from our new home. We are Breezepack. Stormpack does not know this after the many years we have worked together." Moonheart looked momentarily stunned. "What do you mean, 'after the many years we have worked together?'" Sunnystorm chuckled. "In a time when your mother was Alpha and I was a mere Recruit, dogs, and wolves lived in harmony. But I shall not get into detail."

"But–" Moonheart stuttered. "Moonheart, I would like you to help Graycloud gather a patrol to meet the wolves at the border. I will meet you there. I have something I must take care of before I go."

And without another word, she left the den with Rose hard on her heels.

CHAPTER 17

Almost half of the pack was moving swiftly through the forest. Graycloud and Sunnystorm were at the head of the group, throwing instructions behind them. Talonfoot, Thornstripe, Winterpelt, Boltwing, and Skystar were in the middle while taking up the rear were Blazefang, Moonheart, and Nightriver.

As they approached the river, Moonheart was hit with the scent of many wolves. Sure enough, it looked like the whole of Stormpack was gathered at the river. "Well, Sunnystorm, nice to see you again," Stormfoot growled. Sunnystorm approached the edge of the river. "You wanted a fight? Well, here we are!"

A howl rang through the forest as the wolves charged through the water. The dogs charged toward them. Moonheart found herself cornered by three wolves. She looked around desperately and found a large rock a little way off.

"I've tasted dog before," laughed a wolf half the size of Stormfoot, "but never have I tasted a half-breed." The wolf crouched, ready to leap, and the other two advanced. But Moonheart was ready for them. The biggest of the wolves pounced and she rolled over onto her back, kicking as hard as she could. It must have worked because there was a yelp and the wolf fell to the ground with a thud, whimpering. With the way now cleared, she ran through the two remaining wolves and towards the rock. Everything was chaotic. Thornstripe was fighting two wolves at a time while a little way off Blazefang was fighting an elder.

"Where are you?" Moonheart whispered to herself. Sunnystorm was nowhere to be seen. Graycloud had broken his paw and was pinned down by Stormfoot. "No!" Moonheart yelled as she dashed for them. She never made it though. Moments after she had started running, she was bowled over by the same wolf she had just fought. "It's over, pup. Do you hear me? It's over!"

And with a triumphant howl, he lunged for her neck.

+++

"Moonheart! You must wake up!" Moonheart blinked. She was surrounded by the four glowing stones. Silverstone's blue glowing outline towered over her.

"Wha—"

Moonheart slowly stood up. "What's going on? Where is everyone?" Silverstone walked slowly around her daughter. "They are still fighting while you are still gaining your life back."

Moonheart stood still for a moment before shouting, "BUT I NEED TO GET BACK! MY FRIENDS COULD BE DYING RIGHT NOW AND I'M WASTING TIME TALKING TO YOU!"

Silverstone winced and Moonheart immediately regretted shouting. Then a question popped into her head. "What do you mean, gaining my life back?"

Silverstone stopped pacing and stared at Moonheart. "You were born under the full moon, and you are Half-breed. This gives you the power to come back to life when dead. But only five times. So far, you have died twice now."

Moonheart looked at her mother. "That's why I come here whenever something like that happens. I'm just gaining my life back." Silverstone nodded and raised her head so that her snout pointed at the star-filled sky. "It is time for you to go back to battle."

"Wait!" Moonheart yelped as Silverstone began to fade away. Then everything went black. It felt like she was being squeezed. She was afraid to inhale breath in case she suffocated. Then it all stopped. She was back in the battle.

Sunnystorm leaped over Moonheart and straight towards Stormfoot who was laughing maniacally while fighting Thornstripe. Moonheart stifled a gasp as she saw that Graycloud was sprawled out on the ground a little way off. "Moonheart! You're ok!"

Blazefang ran over to her with Talonfoot right behind him. "We thought you were, you know, dead." Talonfoot whimpered. "Don't worry though," Blazefang added, "that wolf that attacked you will never sink his teeth into another piece of meat. Boltwing took care of that."

Moonheart flicked her tail over to where Thornstripe and Sunnystorm were attempting to overtake Stormfoot.

Talonfoot and Blazefang nodded in unison and together all three of them crouched down in the grass. Moonheart remembered the first time she was stalking prey with her friends. How this all started with one little hunting party.

Moonheart flicked her tail to Blazefang to take the right side of Stormfoot and nodded to Talonfoot to take the left. Moonheart padded up the middle. *This is it.* Moonheart thought. *I must end this. If I die doing it, so be it. As long as my pack can live to tell the tale. But maybe there will be a chance we survive this. Then I can talk to Talonfoot and maybe spend time with Blazefang...*

Moonheart stared up at Stormfoot who was so focused on Sunnystorm and Thornstripe that he did not notice the three dogs who were about to ambush him. Then, taking in a final glance at the beautiful forest she called home and all the dogs she called friends, she leaped after Stormfoot.

CHAPTER 18

As Moonheart suspected, Stormfoot did not see them coming. Blazefang had leaped onto his back and was sinking his teeth into his flesh. Talonfoot was clawing at his side while Moonheart took the other. With the five dog's combined strength, they were able to bring Stormfoot to the ground. "No!" He shouted. He writhed on the blood-stained ground, but it was no use. Moonheart had already sunk her teeth into his neck.

After a while Stormfoot's attempts to get free were getting weaker and before long, he stopped completely. Moonheart slowly let go, panting heavily. Then, there was an uproar of cheers and howls. "You did it Moonheart!" Said Blazefang, leaping up beside her on top of Stormfoot.

Moonheart was beginning to take the praise when she realized that Sunnystorm was not in the group. She was by a tree stump where the old body of Graycloud lay, motionless. A wail caught in Moonheart's throat as she bounded across the clearing to Sunnystorm's side.

"He was my friend," she whispered. Moonheart nodded. "He was all of our friends." Sunnystorm nodded and stood up. She suddenly looked older than she was. "Graycloud always said he wanted to be buried on the battlefield. Nightriver, Thornstripe, see to that."

The two dogs nodded and immediately got to work digging the grave. "Winterpelt and Blazefang, patrol the border to see if we got the last of the wolves. The rest of you, follow me back to camp."

+++

Once they arrived back at camp, Sunnystorm rushed to her den. Speck trotted out of the den looking grim. "What's going on?" She asked once she reached Moonheart. "Why is everyone so sad? Did we win?" Moonheart nodded. Speck looked at her Trainer carefully. "Who did we lose?" She asked. "Graycloud. Stormfoot killed him."

Speck whimpered and dashed back to her den. Moonheart decided to go and visit Hazel. But when she peeked into the den, she was nowhere to be seen. *Probably in Sunnystorm's den.* Moonheart thought. But for some reason, she wanted to avoid Sunnystorm for a while.

The sun was setting by the time Winterpelt and Blazefang returned. Nightriver and Thornstripe followed not long after. Spotting her, Blazefang dashed over to greet her with a lick on the ear. "Cheer up, Moonheart. He may be dead, but he's safe with your mother now."

Moonheart felt tears build up in her eyes. Sensing this, Blazefang dipped his head and backed off toward the prey pile.

Sunnystorm was now exiting her den with Bluepetal, Thornstripe, Rose, and Hazel following her. Sunnystorm bounded to the center of the camp and howled. HoweverHowever,, it wasn't necessary because everyone was already gathered. "As you all probably already know, Graycloud is gone. We will need a new Beta." Sunnystorm closed her eyes and took a breath. "The new Beta of the pack shall be Moonheart."

For a moment, Moonheart was stunned. *She must have made a mistake,* she thought. After a moment's silence, the pack burst into cheers. Speck had dashed up to her followed by Talonfoot and Blazefang. "My Trainer's the Beta!" Speck shouted excitedly. Blazefang had tackled Moonheart, laughing. "I knew it! I knew one day you'd be the Beta."

Sunnystorm padded up to the four dogs. There was a smile spread across her face. She signaled to her den and Moonheart nodded. Then realization struck her. She would no longer be able to sleep in the Roamer's den.

As Moonheart pushed her way into the den, a new smell surprised her. Growling, she pounced at the wolf laying on Sunnystorm's bedding. "Moonheart, let me explain first," Sunnystorm growled before Moonheart could close her teeth around the wolf's leg. As she did, she realized this wolf was no stranger. It was Mistwhisper.

"Hello again, Moonheart." She said respectfully. Moonheart stared in awe at the wolf. "She's staying in the pack, isn't she?" She asked. Sunnystorm nodded. "Mistwhisper never liked living with Stormpack. That's why Silverstone helped me get her and Blazefang together."

Moonheart couldn't help but gasp. "That's where you went before you came to battle. You snuck her into camp." Sunnystorm nodded. "Though I would like your permission to let her stay and live among us."

Moonheart stared at Sunnystorm. She was asking for *her* permission to do something. Thinking of Blazefang, she said, "Of course, she can live here. Maybe with her and Thornstripe in the camp, we can make Breezepack like it was before. Wolves and dogs and half-breeds."

Sunnystorm nodded again and signaled for Moonheart and Mistwhisper to follow her out of the den. They found Thornstripe waiting outside of the den looking expressionless. "Sunnystorm." She began but Sunnystorm paid her no attention. Blazefang, Talonfoot, and Speck were gathered by the prey pile. As soon as Blazefang laid eyes on Mistwhisper he nearly jumped out of his skin.

Dashing over to her, he licked her all over. "I missed you so much! I was worried you were in the battle with the wolves." Mistwhisper backed up away from him. "I would never side with them. But guess what? I'm part of Breezepack now!"

Before Blazefang could respond, Skystar was stomping up to them with Frost padding behind her. "Sunnystorm, you can't let her live here. She's a wolf!" Thornstripe stepped up in front of Skystar. "I'm a wolf, you don't have a problem with me." She growled. "You've had plenty of time to show your loyalty to the pack!"

"Then in time, Mistwhisper shall do the same. Until then, you will treat her with respect."

Skystar glared at Thornstripe for a while longer before stalking toward the Roamer's den. Mistwhisper looked down at her paws and muttered, "Thank you." Thornstripe gave a quick little nod and walked away towards the Roamer's den.

Sunnystorm now looked at Moonheart. "Don't you think you should be preparing the hunting patrols?" Moonheart nodded and looked at Blazefang. "Can you lead a patrol with Boltwing and Frost?" He nodded vigorously. And lead the chosen dogs to the entrance.

CHAPTER 19

The next few months were peaceful now that the wolves were gone. Everyone was cheerful now. Spring was closer than ever. Bright was beginning to grow. Frost was training fast, which Speck did not approve of, and was preparing for her naming ceremony.

Moonheart was just walking into the camp carrying a squirrel when she heard Sunnystorm call, "Breezepack! Gather around for a meeting!"

Speck came running down the tunnel behind Moonheart with a rabbit dangling from her jaws. When she spotted Frost strutting proudly up to Sunnystorm, she groaned.

"Frost has trained for many moons now," she was saying, "and is ready to become a Roamer."

There was silence as Sunnystorm looked down on Frost, who was shaking with excitement. "Frost, you will now be known as Frostclaw."

A great cheer rose from the gathered dogs as Frostclaw dipped her head respectfully to Sunnystorm. Despite her annoyance of not becoming a Roamer, Speck dashed to Frostclaw's side shouting, "This is my sister! She's a Roamer now!"

Winterpelt and Boltwing licked their daughter proudly. Moonheart caught sight of Skystar smiling to herself at the back of the crowd. Sunnystorm silenced the dogs with a flick of her tail. "I would also like to name another trainer today."

Her blue eyes searched the gathered dogs until they landed on Speck. "Me?" She exclaimed. Sunnystorm nodded, and Speck padded excitedly to the front of the crowd.

"Speck, I have thought long and hard about what to name you. You have shown great bravery countless times, including the battle with the wolves."

Realization struck Moonheart. It hadn't been Boltwing that had saved her from the wolf, it had been Speck.

"Speck, I would like to name you Speckbreeze." They howled their approval and Speckbreeze raised her head proudly. Frostclaw nuzzled her sister affectionately. "This is my sister! She's a Roamer now," she whispered into Speckbreeze's ear.

Sunnystorm signaled with her tail that the meeting was over and bounded over to Bluepetal. Moonheart noticed that Blazefang was sneaking out of the camp entrance. She began to call him but stopped. She wanted to see what he was up to.

She signaled to Speckbreeze, who was now heading sleepily towards the Roamer's den, and she bounded to Moonheart's side. Moonheart explained to her about Blazefang, but before she finished Speckbreeze was already halfway through the tunnel. They followed Blazefang's scent to the river. Moonheart was about to wade through it when there was a yowl from nearby.

Her ears pricked, and Speckbreeze sprinted in the direction of the sound. A new scent filled Moonheart's nostrils, and her heart almost stopped when she realized that Blazefang's scent was mingled with it. It was the scent of wolf and blood.

She began to run faster. She ran as fast as her legs would allow. She almost ran into Speckbreeze as she skidded to a stop. Moonheart looked over her shoulder to see Mistwhisper sprawled out on the ground panting heavily. Blazefang sat happily on one side, licking what seemed to be a pup.

"Moonheart!" He gasped as he finally noticed their presence. "Speckbreeze! Come and meet Cloud! I named him after Graycloud. I think he would approve of the name."

Speckbreeze didn't hesitate to pad out into the clearing and sniff Cloud welcomingly. Moonheart hesitated, looking worriedly toward Mistwhisper.

As if reading her thoughts, Blazefang said, "She'll be fine. It took a lot of strength to get him out." Feeling reassured, Moonheart padded into the clearing to gently lick Cloud on the head. Then a concerning thought made Moonheart shiver. "Why did you guys come out here?" Blazefang seemed prepared to answer this question because he answered immediately, "As you already know, Mistwhisper was welcomed into the pack. Everybody's already not that fond of her, so when they hear that she has a pup, imagine how everyone will react."

Moonheart shook her head. "If you guys stay away from Breezepack, they'll never grow fond of her." Blazefang bristled. "I don't care what they think of her. I love her and that's all that matters." He took a breath before continuing. "We're thinking of starting our pack soon."

"What?" Speckbreeze stopped playing with Cloud and looked up at Blazefang. "But there are only three of you!" Blazefang nodded. "There may be only three of us now, but from what Hazel has said, she has two more on the way."

"Hazel knows about this?" Moonheart asked. "Yep. She's the one who finalized our decision." "There may be two more pups on the way," Mistwhisper put in quietly, finally gaining her strength back. "But after that, what will you do?" Speckbreeze asked. "There will only be five in the pack."

"We thought about that too," he said. "We'll let Cloud grow up in camp and find someone who he'll love." Speckbreeze's ear twitched. "There's no one near his age though." Blazefang chuckled. "Not even Rose?"

Speckbreeze glared at Blazefang for a moment longer before settling down next to Cloud, who was now slowly walking around the clearing. "You wouldn't mind staying with us for a little while?" He asked Moonheart. "Of course, we'll stay. I just can't believe you have a pup already!"

She settled down next to Blazefang and watched as Speckbreeze gently fought with Cloud.

CHAPTER 20

After spending the rest of the day with Blazefang, Cloud, and Mistwhisper, Moonheart and Speckbreeze set off for the camp. The sun was sinking below the horizon, and everything was quiet except for the crunch of leaves underfoot and the steady breathing of the two dogs. Moonheart noticed that Speckbreeze did not look as enthusiastic as she did before they left the camp.

"Are you ok?" Moonheart asked her. Speckbreeze whipped around. There was sadness in her amber eyes. "It's nothing. I was just— thinking."

Before Moonheart could press on, Speckbreeze ran through the bushes. Moonheart entered the camp feeling both happy and concerned. Blazefang had started a life with somebody already. With a pang of loneliness, she realized she had not felt what he felt. She gazed around the camp and noticed Talonfoot on his back, resting his eyes. *Or maybe I have,* she thought suddenly. She thought back to all the times Talonfoot talked to her and asked her to hunt. All the times he helped her when she needed it. It turned out she *did* have someone who loved her.

With this thought locked in her brain, she slowly padded up to Talonfoot. He shot open his eyes and looked up into hers. "Hey Moonheart!" He yapped. "I was wondering where you went. What's up?" Moonheart looked into his green eyes and took a deep breath. "Talonfoot, could I talk to you for a second?"

He jumped up and followed Moonheart to the corner of the camp, near the entrance. She was aware of Speckbreeze's gaze burning her fur all the way. "Talonfoot," Moonheart began, "I think I finally know how I feel about you. I hope I'm not making the wrong decision by telling you this, but I love you. I don't know how I haven't realized this before, but I do."

Talonfoot blinked. "I— I don't know what to say. Moonheart, of course, I love you. I've loved you for a long time now. I'm glad you told me this."

He licked Moonheart on the head and headed toward the Roamer's den. She suddenly felt so much lighter now that she had told him that. She was about to call Speckbreeze over when she quickly got up and headed toward her sister who was sharing a vole with Skystar.

Feeling disappointed, she grabbed a starling from the pile and headed to a log. Winterpelt was grooming her fur. She stopped and looked up at Moonheart. "Hello, Moonheart." Moonheart sat down beside her and tore into her prey. Winterpelt looked over at Speckbreeze then back at Moonheart. "What's going on between you two? When you left the camp, everything was fine. Then Speckbreeze came back before you looking upset. What's going on?"

Moonheart tried to focus on her prey, but her mind lingered on this question. What had happened between them? Why was Speckbreeze suddenly avoiding her?

"I don't know," Moonheart said simply. Winterpelt looked like she was going to say more but before she could, Moonheart jumped up and went to the den. Talonfoot was at the back of the den sleeping. Cometfire neatly laid a new moss bed for Nightriver before she settled down in it. She nodded to Moonheart before curling up and falling asleep.

Moonheart silently said hello to Cometfire before turning her sleep circles and laying down next to Talonfoot. The warmth of his fur comforted her, and she soon drifted off to sleep.

✦✦✦

Moonheart blinked sleep from her eyes. Moonlight was pouring through the entrance of the den. The den was empty. She got up and peeked her head out of the den. The only sound was the rustling of leaves. Where was everybody?

Suddenly, there was a hissing sound from behind her and she whirled around. Standing there was a figure slightly smaller than she was. "Who are you?" She asked. The figure did not reply. More figures like it appeared out of the shadows, hissing fiercely. Then the scent of Silverstone flooded over her, and she saw her mother sitting atop a boulder.

"Do you see this, Moonheart?" She said, her voice amplified so it could be heard throughout the forest. "This is what is to come. They will tear the pack apart.

Unless you stop it. Gather four until there are three. This is the dog's destiny. In this battle, others will fall. Until the most unlikely will beat them all. You must rise against this foe, or our kind will have nowhere to go."

The figures crept closer, hissing and slashing at Moonheart. Silverstone began to fade away. "Wait!" Moonheart called. "Who is this foe?" But it was too late. She could no longer see. She caught a glimpse of striped, orange fur before being clawed at by the figures.

A U T H O R S   B I O

Jared Bailey is a loving son and protective big brother. His desire to be an author at age 11 comes from his passion for reading. Jared can always be found with a book in his hand. It is his hope that following his dreams will inspire other young people to follow theirs.

www.ingramcontent.com/pod-product-compliance
Lightning Source LLC
Chambersburg PA
CBHW071441130726
47997CB00006B/2179